Chapel of Inadvertent Joy

Pitt Poetry Series
Ed Ochester, Editor

CHAPEL OF INADVERTENT JOY

JEFFREY MᶜDANIEL

UNIVERSITY OF PITTSBURGH PRESS

Published by the University of Pittsburgh Press, Pittsburgh, Pa., 15260

Copyright © 2013, Jeffrey McDaniel

Manufactured in the United States of America

Printed on acid-free paper

10 9 8 7 6 5 4 3 2 1

ISBN 13: 978-0-8229-6260-1

ISBN 10: 0-8229-6260-8

for Alexander Jutkowitz, who signed my tenth-grade yearbook:

Keep up the poetry . . .
just don't read it to me anymore.

I shall lead you, as a guest from another country,
to the Chapel of Inadvertent Joy,

where dark-gold domes shine,
and the bells of sleeplessness roar.

There, from the burgundy clouds,
the mother of god will drop her flimsy coat

and you will rise, ripe with power,
never ashamed that you have loved me.

—Marina Tsvetaeva

CONTENTS

Little Soldier of Love

Reflections of a Cuckold and Other Blasphemies

Return to *El Mundo Perdido*

Chapel of Inadvertent Joy

Little Soldier of Love

Hello

The person gazing at this page before you had really amazing eyes—
blue the way the Caribbean is blue that first minute off the plane

to someone who grew up in Jersey. Anyway, it's good you're here.
The truth is I've been lonely, crawling up and down the page at night.

Life is like this boomerang: you get hurled out, and everything
is fresh, then you hit forty, start to arc back to the hand

that flung you from the womb, the Lord's hand, and then
it's all rerun. I know I'm complaining, and that it's unattractive,

but please, forgive me, because complaining is like sex for old people.
Have you ever cringed with your whole body? Been so filled with shame

you wanted to wriggle out of your flesh, like a serpent in a forest,
like the snake that betrayed Eve? No one ever mentions

how the snake apologized, how he tried to make it up to them,
how the Lord punished the snake too, said *I will fill your kind*

with so much shame and self-hatred you will writhe out of yourself
every six months, just like a man's penis. It's true—twice a year

men wake and find nothing in their boxers, but the empty casings
of their runaway fallacies. Anyway, 1875, a Civil War vet from Virginia

gets off a boat in England. Everyone calls him *Yankee*. He cringes, snarls
I ain't no Yankee. I killed Yankees, but after a month he begins to take it,

the way we all begin to take the gray hairs in our underpants, the ring
of our anus loosening, our rocket ship struggling to pierce

the atmosphere. Now, if you would just lean forward a little, friend,
and drag your fragrant strands over my voluptuous grief.

Track of Now

It's one of those days when you can hear everyone's heart beating,
      can feel the blood trickling through people's veins.
I feel so fertile—each woman in Tompkins Square Park
      eats her ice cream just for me.
Trees shimmer and swell in their bark.
I have guitar strings in my throat and flamenco the mother
      hauling three children in a stroller.
I see the vein in the haystack of the junkie's arm.
I feel people across town thinking about me, can sense myself blooming
      in Molly's mind like a desert rose.
Old people gather around the dog park and look at the hounds
      that had been their youth.
I can see the smile being passed from face to face, like a baton,
      as we glide around the track of now.
Even the cosmic amputee feels three-quarters whole.
Joan Wasser sings under an oak tree, her voice so fierce and luminous,
      like watching glass being blown.
Young women float by in dresses made from the skin of green apples.
A businessman drools his boozy initials onto the blouse of a Polish teenager.
Everyone's genital odometer is wiped clean.
So this is what it feels like to have sex with the universe, I think,
as a pigeon lands on my shoulder and whispers
      tomorrow's winning lotto number in my ear.

A Brief History of the Future

There will be traffic clones with glow-in-the-dark eyes
that live under intersections and only pop up
when the power sputters to a halt.

You'll be able to adjust the sound of your heartbeat
like the ring of a cell phone.

After a night of heavy drinking, you'll peel your face off
and send it to the cleaners to have the wrinkles steamed out.

There'll be virtual amusement parks
where you can drown in the milk of your first lover's thighs.

When you have a feeling, you'll be able to push a *here* button
so you'll always know how to get back.

Regular memory will begin to look like an old, beat-up car.

Parents will sneak into their children's brains at night
and examine the raw footage.

Instead of churches, we'll have giant radios
with huge metallic antennas for steeples.
If you sit on the coils, you can listen to god
with your entire body, as his holy broadcast ricochets
off the aluminum walls of your bloodstream.

Beware of the Dark Sedan Idling Inside You

I flick a switch—out flashes the lightbulb,
like God snapping his fingers in my face:
Wake up, Pumpkinhead. I've been running around
half-naked, with the rest of America,
wearing only a credit card and a cashmere scarf.
Arf, arf. Yesterday, I went to Circuit City's
going-out-of-business sale to revel in the fall of capitalism,
but all I saw were the sad faces of underpaid workers.

Welcome to land of the free fall
and the freebaser, as well as the freelancer
and freeloader, and front-loading washing machine,
where you can empty your conscience and wash
all those illicit thoughts about illegal immigrants
out of your brain, where it's still ok
to dock your canoe at the racist joke island
at cocktail parties and chuckle. Two housewives
bang prescription medicine bottles
and whisper *cheers.* An hour opens
its trench coat and shows you its stolen minutes.
A homeless man gets a boner while sleeping
on a steam grate. There's a dark car idling
inside you. The question is: do you get in?

Attention, Please

Ladies and gentlemen, your life is located
under your sofa cushions. In the event
of an emergency, slip your life
over your head. Connect the clip
and tighten by pulling outward. To inflate
your life, yank the red tabs firmly down.
To inflate your life further, blow
into the mouthpiece. In case of depression,
life masks will automatically drop
from the compartments above. Place
the life mask over your nose
and mouth. Pull the elastic strap.
Remain calm and breathe. Your life
supply is now regulated. It is normal
that the life mask does not fully inflate.

Happy Marriage

You're sitting on the sofa. Your husband
is upstairs, your child sleeping. There are dishes
in the sink with your name on them. A dark sedan
pulls up to the curb of your mind. You know
you should turn and run the other way.
But you don't. You stand there.
The blackened rear window rolls down.
It's a boy you knew in high school, holding a rose.
The door opens. You climb in.
Your husband upstairs doesn't hear the car pull away.
In the dark sedan, there's a replica of the boy's room:
        balled-up gym socks on the floor.
You climb onto the sheet-less mattress.
His mouth roves over you like a searchlight.
Through the blackened windows, you see
        your husband come down the stairs.
He's holding a dirty plate with your name on it.
You bend your knees and pull your legs back.
A movie of this moment is being projected
        onto the vinyl ceiling.
Your chest fills with runaway breath.
The sedan accelerates around a corner.
Your husband calls you into the kitchen.
His words like a leash around your neck.
You straighten up, walk over.
The tremor in your shoulder is the echo
        of the boy galloping inside you.

Eliot Spitzer in Grad School

The fortune cookie says: *the spotlight*
will cradle you like a surrogate mother. Lord,
swaddle me with a blanket dipped in smallpox
so I can feel indigenous sin,
so I can open my mouth and bite
into the snake's Adam's apple. All this talk
of destiny, but what I want to know is
how it felt for Abe Lincoln
to be six years old, dumping out
a jar of pennies on the log-cabin floor.
Did he notice anything familiar
about the bearded man staring back at him?
Do we only recognize our fate
when it grabs us by the collar
like a train conductor and shakes us awake
on the 7:45 White Plains local, saying *sir,*
this is your stop. This really is your stop.
How many of us ignore fate's hand
brushing our cheeks and tumble
back into slumber? One side of a coin says:
you will do great things in your lifetime.
The other side reads: *you will rain shame*
upon your family. I flip the coin in the air,
as if only one of them can be true.

The Cougar Tree

Have you no shame, tree, ripping your leaves off
like a green dress at a barbecue? You're not
an April chicken anymore: tooth marks on your branches
where the woodchucks nibbled your skinny limbs.

I hear you at night, tree, drunkenly purring towards the sky,
wiggling your twigs at birds winging south for winter,
hey sailor, want to rest those weary feathers? In another life,
you're a zillion toothpicks, a millennium of ax handles.

In another life, you're an all-season diner for termites,
an umbrella's wiry skeleton for teenagers in love.
But in this life, trunk splitting into dual leaders, feuding
torsos, you press against your bark dress, and the truth is,

I envy you: how you shrug off the wind's gossip, broadcast
every grainy inch of your brittle, bodacious self.

A Brief History of Eyebrows

Kate Winslet's eyebrows
are the arms of an Olympic swimmer
in the last length of the butterfly.

The devil's eyebrows
are knitted from the nose hairs of infants.

Winona Ryder's eyebrows are safety pins
holding her face together.

The fieldworker's eyebrows
are sweat rags stitched
directly into his forehead.

John Keats's eyebrows
are two maple coffins
being carried across a field of snow.

And your eyebrows are church benches
I want to be carved into like initials.

The Barbecued Man

Orange flashes through the hole where the windshield used to be.
A splatter of volcanic splotches, like drops of scorched milk,

sears into the Pompei of his cheeks. Days later, he dreams his parents
are part snake, so he might writhe free of this charred translucence.

Doctors compact a chin from sashimi-thin slices of gut, twine and dye
ruby lips from forearm slivers. And voila: a face. He has nightmares

of a crowded lunchtime street, a gust of wind lifting
his new face away, like a silk tissue, hand reaching up,

people gawking at the hooks dangling from his scalp, arteries
flailing like tassels. *I am the barbecued man, here to cook you alive.*

I will hold you to the lit coals that are my eyes, and hurl your prayers
into the furnace of my mouth, where smoulder is a verb, adjective, noun.

Pity Party

Invite the woman
who lost her husband
in the flickering hands

of flame. And the man
whose arm was chewed up
by a jaw of shrapnel.

And the colonel
whose son strapped himself
to the ceiling fan and took

a breezy leap of faith.
And the father who croons
lullabies for his five-year-old

as buckshot spackles
the window pane. Have each
prepare a few words

about suffering, but make sure
each ends by testifying
that my woes put

their woes in perspective,
that my woes are, in fact,
the measuring stick.

The Grudge

I watered the grudge,
not with the fervent devotion
of a nun clutching rosary beads,
not with the destructive clockwork
of a drunk spilling vodka
tumblers on the cactus erupting
through his heart, but I watered it,
went out there at midnight,
with a can of spittle, moon dangling
like a lightbulb from its frail cord,
and I dripped the dark
nourishing fluid into its roots,
my face pulsing like a blister
as the venom petals bloomed.

Pick-up Lines of the Marquis de Sade

Come back to my oubliette,
I'll renovate your self-esteem,
let you suckle my clarinet
dipped in candle wax and gasoline.

Want a light, my glittery darkness?
I'll make your tendons quiver.
Blindfold you with a road map to Hades
and tickle your jingle bells with a razor.

Want me to locate the hymen
in your psyche, misses?
I'll tap that lacy-thin flap of brain skin
with a mallet and pinprick kisses.

I'll pop drops of your blood
like Percodans at a suicide bash.
Just recline inside my stretch crucifix
fueled by the skin off your ass.

Conditionals

If you can't take the heat, stay out of the kitchen
If you can't take the kitsch, stay out of the gift shop
If you can't take the guillotine, stay out of the guilt
If you can't take the guilt trip, stay out of the narrative
If you can't take the narcissism, stay out of the mirror
If you can't take the miracle, stay out of the mire
If you can't take the mirage, stay out of the desert
If you can't take the desecration, stay out of the bedroom
If you can't take the bedlam, stay out of the pillbox
If you can't take the pills, stay out of the plunder
If you can't take the plunge, stay out of the chapel
If you can't take the chatter of teeth, stay out of the freezer
If you can't take the freestyle, stay out of the cipher
If you can't take the sci-fi, stay out of the Spielberg
If you can't take the spiel, stay out of the showroom
If you can't take the shove, stay out of the accusation
If you can't take the ache, stay out of the land belonging to the heart

Little Soldier of Love

March, you were just here.
Now you're gone, vanished,
on permanent hiatus. A month
of rain you were. A month
of me strapped to an ottoman
in a hotel room, blindfolded,
you snapping pictures of me naked,
then posting them on Craigslist,
asking *who wants her now*. The ticking
of the clock, the chilled steam
from your lung machine, the knock
on the door, the heavy footsteps,
the anonymous canisters
of breath exploding
on my shoulder, a sweaty
palm on my calf, a zipper
opening so slowly, each metal
notch catching on the ridges
of my spine. March,
think you can just order
room service and leave me
bed-tied, a note taped
to my clavicle? Every year
it's the same with you: marching
muddy footprints through people's lives,
little door with rusty hinges
to the forehead opened wide.

Satan Exulting Over Eve

after a color-print drawing by William Blake

Here she is, master, your little child.
See how her head slopes back, neck arched,
as if frozen in prayer, hair spilling
out of her skull in thick, amber waves,
as wisdom's venom courses through her. See
how my scaly logic coils around her,
like bacon curling a lush piece of shrimp.
Come and get her, lord,
before I throw her on the grill.

Oh, don't act so surprised—you knew
this would happen, dressing up
your little mousetrap like paradise,
with sycamores and starlings,
dipping sweet Eve's tresses in jasmine,
rubbing crushed lilac between her toes
and setting her here like bait,
her fragrance loose in the wind.

You knew I was coming, lord.
You put the ticking in the apple. You placed
the fatal in the fruit. I, your slithering assassin,
your eternal patsy, merely carried out
your grimiest deed with reptilian loyalty,
so you could hero in under a balcony of stars
that always seem to depict you in a positive light.

What?! You deny it? Is the court to believe
you're almighty in every way but this?
That even with crystal balls for pupils,
and binoculars in your fingertips
you could not foresee this?
Now you hide up there behind a sunbeam,
muttering *free will*. Ha! Heavily
discounted perhaps, but never free.

Oh, but you should've seen it, father—
how I took my time, found a little knob
in Eve's mind and turned the temptation
up slow, till desire began to fill her
like gasoline in the belly of a boat,
starting with just one plump, purple drop,
then another, then her hull sagging,
her mouth opening. Oh, father,
just as perception trickled out of her
like the last slur of wine from a kicked over bottle,
I whispered, *Dear Eve, I had to do it,
without you, I'm not Satan—just a squandered angel.
Now I'm the inventor of heaven.*

But, oh, my liege, I wish you could've seen her
tighten her grip around that *Malus pumila*
and ruthlessly test the apple's ripeness
with a brush of her incisors—all that forbidden
knowledge about to carnival into her psyche.

She knew what she was doing, master,
her eyes like caramel simmering,
as her lips parted, cheeks hollowing
inward to a glove, her molars
sinking into me the apple, groaning.

I am all maple now:
skull tilted back, sinister high notes
shuddering into the dark, nethery spires
of my temples, irises quivering
like the quartz tips of metronomes,
as melted coins of moonlight
jukebox out of me.

How could something so pure and sweet
have sprung from the gypsy cauldron of my loins?

What's that? Now you make threats
to line her pelvis with matchstick-sized grenades
so, when her offspring grinds out,
pain will ricochet through her hips
like shrapnel, till she screams your name
in labor? Talk about vanity.
Some savior you are—saving her
for yourself perhaps, you two-faced swine,
planting and pruning the tree of death
beside the tree of life. Yes, I am evil.
Yes, I am the minister of woe,
but at least I'm consistent.

And what about Adam—you're boy wonder,
with all those ribs? Well, he climbed
the tree of curiosity, father, and he watched
thimbles of Eve's breath lap
the shoreline of my forearm. Now he wants
to grow up to be just like me, Uncle Lucifer,
the one who cracks darkness in two
and extracts light. Her gasps,
like pink balloons leaving the hands
of children, floating up
into the never-ending space
between my ears: *tremolo,*
tremolo, tremolo.

Yes, my lord, you are infinite. Yes,
you control the galaxies, but this space
here between the shoulder blades
is mine. I patrol this orb, this throb
of fruit plucked from the celestial tree
and spun here recklessly.
This bruised orchard is mine.

Keeper of the Light

I fork rice and breakfast beans into my mouth. Gnaw
a slither of beef, rough as a donkey's ear, then wash it down

with boxed apple juice. Read the paper on the sofa.
My job doesn't start till the sun drops

to its knees and fires pink arrows into the bellies
of clouds. Only then do I climb the two hundred stairs,

spiraling up through the guts of the tower,
that from a distance in daylight looks like a brick telescope

wedged into the ground. Only then do I load the lamp
with whale oil, and trim the wick so it burns evenly

like a red beard across a pirate's face. Only then do I scrub
the layer of carbon off the reflectors and adjust

the Fresnel lens, which is like a lampshade made out of shards
of an expensive mirror, harnessing the many stems of light

into a bouquet to be hurled out, in three second intervals.
Only then do I turn the shortwave to the chatter

of ships. Only then, binoculars round my neck,
do I slide open the door and walk the rail,

a salty breeze curling through my pores, as I comb
the dark waves with my eyes. Flag whipping

overhead. Thunder cooking in clouds.
Then the voices start rumbling in. I read you

thirteen-year-old girl pinned down by your friend's
nineteen-year-old brother in a basement and excavated

as your favorite Crosby, Stills & Nash song
plays cruelly over the speakers. I read you housewife

with a crushed starfish in your belly, clutching
a wine glass like a buoy. I cannot promise

help is on the way, but I read you high school senior,
razor marks ricocheting up your forearm. I read you

husband watching school after school of naughty minnows
swim across the screen of your smart phone, as the rain gathers

around your ankles in the matrimonial rowboat. I read you
thirty-year-old woman, smearing kerosene over your breasts,

like baby oil, a carousel of men assembling, jerking up
and down, like warped horses on a misery-go-round. I read you

friend from childhood, counting the petals of a daisy, *I kill me,*
I kill me not. I read you dockworker, wandering

the corridors under the ocean's surface,
stuffing your unemployment check into the belly button

of a slot machine. I read you sixteen-year-old girl,
getting jabbed with the *t* in the word *slut*

as you tremble on the train platform and lean back
into the broad metal arms of eternity. I read you

and chart your coordinates. Note your howls. And no,
I cannot save you, or bring supplies—just sit inside

this giant candle and fling thimbles of light
in your direction, whispering, *I hear you, hold tight.*

Reflections of a Cuckold and Other Blasphemies

In the middle of my journey through life,
I came to my senses in a dark forest,
the righteous path nowhere in sight.

—DANTE

The Birds and the Bees

When I hit thirteen, the noun between my legs
turning into a verb, my father sat me down and said:

one day you will have a wife of your own. A man
will come—a helpful neighbor knocking

while you're at work perhaps, or a garlicky colleague
at an office party, or a lifeguard on a spit of sand—

and that man will grip your beloved, perhaps
even in your sheets, but that won't mean you're weak.

Remember our great ancestor, Menelaus, triceps
the size of grapefruits, his chest far hairier

than that slim-hipped boy who slipped in and swiped
his wife, like a calla lily from his lapel. Remember

Marcus Aurelius' words: *reject your sense of injury
and the injury itself disappears.* No need to launch

another Trojan, just because some stallion
trotted into her. No need to perish like Pushkin

slumped in ice. Begin preparing now. When friends
sleep over, let them colonize your bed. Never yell

shotgun—the backseat will scrub you down,
so years later, when your wife stumbles home

with that glazed, seen-god look in her eyes, the sweat
of his trigger-happy fingers still greasing the white

napkin of her thighs, you can settle into that moment,
ask her how it was, if you can witness next time.

I Am Not an Idiot

I know what happened at the bar:
me and your pal Jake from college
on stools, sipping tall boys, you smiling
between us, the dutiful wife, rubbing

the notches in my spine. I know
he was scribbling cave paintings
onto your thigh, tingles crackling
under your skirt, shorter
than summer in Alaska. I know

later at home, you poured
three thick fingers of cognac,
so he was too boozed to drive,
had to crash on the pullout.

I know you hurried me into the Jacuzzi
of your mouth, just to drowsy me,
that after I exploded, you padded down,
with my bouquet on your breath,
and held open your butterfly wings.

I know his crushed pearls were drying
on your skin, when you tiptoed in
with dawn, the reverb of his olive fingers
still sprinting through your hair.

The Furies

Oh kindly ones, with eyes soft
      as panda fur, and hair
that supplies its own rough breeze,
      would you like a nibble
of this tart, baked with scraps
      of stray dog heart?
There's a fracture in my chimney,
      a crack rippling through
my wedding ring. Twice
      a week, my wife brings
back the soil from another man's
      flowerbed. I wonder
if you might speak with him
      in your language of fire,
one he seems to both play with
      and comprehend.

The Cuckold in Autumn

Raking leaves in sweats a size too big,
my wife's Pinto not in the driveway,
when the neighbor's smug son
struts by with his second girlfriend
of the season. I don't lift my face
from the wrinkled shards of yellow:
a dried-up broken mirror
reflecting my true, discarded self.
They slide into the bucket seats
of his Chevy. *Click. Click.*
The engine won't flip. She emerges,
gaping zeroes in her sockets.
He shuffles towards me, mumbles
something about a jump. My loins
ignite like a furnace. *Welcome
to my world*, I think, attaching cables
under the sprung hood, revving the juice.

Life as a Donkey

In a dream, I'm tapping
my fingers on the dinner table,
the clock ticking: *no wife,*
no wife, no wife, when the Miller
from Canterbury emerges,
ale on his breath, whispers:
learn to accept the stripe
that will appear on your back,
as if your hair can sense
what your mind can't grasp.
Tell yourself that the stripe
in your coarse fur is from Jesus
riding you into Bethlehem,
that a child who straddles you
in his youth will never suffer
a toothache, that the weight
on your back is anything
but your wife and him
nibbling grapes.

Holiday Weekend

He's dragging his Mediterranean tongue
around the perimeter of my wife's lullaby,
like Hector's body around the gates of Troy.

She's arching off the bed, learning to speak
with her hips, saying: *drink from this ceramic
bowl, Achilles.* I whimper, *Helen, don't,*

into the strip of cloth wedged between my teeth.
The worst part is not how my hands are cuffed
to the spindles of the antique rocking chair

we picked out together. The worst part is not
the O her mouth makes as he tugs brightly
colored moans out of her, like hundred-dollar

pashmini scarves, or the bedsprings
rattle like wedding rings shaken in a tin can.
No, the worst part is my own body

betraying me, my heart clanging in time
with their rhythm, and how cozy I am playing
second fiddle in the soundtrack of my life.

The Cuckold Explores the Subjunctive

If I were a flag, I'd be Japan:
the white of surrender
with a red throb in the center.
If I was a fruit, I'd be uneaten.
If I was money, I'd be unearned.
If I were an organization, I'd be the UN.
If I were a pronoun, I'd be them.
If I were a fluid, I'd be smuggled rum.
In a missile fight, I bring a gun.
If I was a point, I'd be moot.
If I were a tree part, I'd be the hard root.
Hard as I watched, hard as I listened.
Hard as he leaned, hard as she twisted.
Hard as he roared, hard as she glistened.
Hard as the price I paid for this wisdom.

Reflections of a Cuckold and Other Blasphemies

It wasn't till she motioned me over
to the barstool to meet the guys
that the ceiling started to spin,
like a carousel gone wrong, helium
hissing in my head, kiss-shaped
bruises radiating outward
from the choked purse
of my scrotum. All night
they charted and recharted
her insatiable constellations.
At dawn, all that was left: a moist
residue where skin had been, a scent
in the air, like barbecued water.

Lust in Translation

When she answers the phone in the middle of the night
    then disappears with three scarves and a bull whip

When I am blindfolded in the corner, and she is the sound
    of a zipper being undone

When my ears are seashells filled with her oceanic moans

When I am a lamp she sticks in the basement

When her chair is empty at the breakfast table

When she leads me by the nose through a briar patch
    on a barbed-wire leash

When she takes off her panties in the front seat
    just before entering the shoe store

When she holds my wrist and presses the lighter into my palm
    and whispers *this is what it feels like—this this this*

The Cuckold and the Penal System

If there was a police lineup
and your shoulder the only witness,
would it be able to select my hand
from all the other hands?

from *The Cuckold's Survivor Manual*

When you decide to rearrange your life
and find that a neighbor has left footprints
on your wife's carpet, don't despair.
Lay down a wet towel, folded in two,
and steam it gently with a hot iron.
If that fails, use a felt-tip pen
and treat the bare threads individually.
Remember: the more often a rug is shaken,
the longer it will live. Dirt trapped
underneath grinds down the threads.

The Cuckold Sees the Bigger Picture

In chimpanzee tribes, three or four males
handle the majority of the mating.
I collect leaves. I guard the perimeter.

What's comforting about a hierarchy
is not being on top, but rather
knowing your place in it.

The Cuckold Contemplates the Malibu Fires

The fire chooses the coastline
because it enjoys its own reflection,
its thousand licking tongues lashing
across the rippling hips of the sea.
The moon's borrowed light suddenly
seems inferior. The fire whispers
to the moon: *See how your woman
writhes for me?* The moon sits stoically,
like a husband, knowing this blast
of passion will pass, that even this luster,
undeniable in its heat, will be gone
in forty-eight hours, and then
it will be moon and ocean again, sharing
an early dinner, before he kisses her
foamy shoulders and rises for work.

Interview with a Cuckold

How do you just sit there and watch
your wife with other men?

*Every man secretly imagines his wife
being passed around a peer group
like a new pair of binoculars
trained on a red-feathered bird.*

So you don't consider it a betrayal?

This whole thing is built on trust.

What is *this* exactly?

A forest of goose bumps.

How long have you been trapped
in this forest?

*My wife is a chainsaw.
She was born to chop wood.*

And what were you born to do?

*I'm the one who sees the tree
fall down in the forest.
I'm the one who makes it real.*

Return to *El Mundo Perdido*

A Brief History of Immortality

The best part was not coming to—in the girl's frilly bed:
flamingo-skinned walls, butterscotch negligee, palm

smearing over her jar of uncapped creaminess, finger
painting the silhouette of a giraffe on her squirming

abdomen, the big wooden bowl of her hips
rising to meet my hungover lips. The best part

was not her mother's eggshell knuckles on the door, *Lily,*
darling, time to go the country, in an English accent,

a minute later, shaking her regal hand, the family dew
surreptitiously licked off (out of respect), though that was

almost the best part. No, the best part was stepping out
of the high-rise elevator into a bright July morning,

89th and Lex, prancing eighty blocks back
to the East Village, a twenty-two-year-old boy from Philly,

with lavender down feathers in his hair and foxy rich girl
nectar in his veins. Taxicabs yielding to his strut,

painted faces on billboards breathing: *boy, your ass*
is like two scoops of vanilla ice cream, with jimmies on top.

Queen of the Shortcuts

Talking with her was like entering a dimly lit room in August
after building sand castles in midday sun: salt in my swim trunks,
fried lotion on my lip, eyes adjusting to her acute darkness. Ah,
to be ten years old again, coming upstairs, finding mother
donkey-eyed, whispering, *there are four ways to find god*, her smile
like a pile of leaves burning from within, *but here is a shortcut*,
lifting her sleeve: a series of bright pink nicks in her forearm.

A Brief History of Neon

First off your bloodstream: 1992,
turquoise minnows swimming cross-eyed,
hypodermic salamanders marooned
on the hourglass beach.

Then '91, her parents' guesthouse,
your activated glow stick pressed
recklessly into her heat lamp,
sending orange butterfly silhouettes
fluttering across the ceiling.

Then '93, a machine gun of red
and blue on the cop car's roof
spraying incandescence across your abdomen,
the cop saying *your eyes are a color*
that doesn't exist in nature.

And to think it all started in '88
with a glassblower who forgot the lit candle
smoldering in her teeth: the flicker
trapped inside a sealed transparent tube,
an elongated firefly, a match
in a constant state of strike.

Return to *El Mundo Perdido*

Touching the limestone of the pyramid's flat roof at noon, I look
      for an indent, a smudge, a fingerprint, some residue of the old me.
Thirteen years ago, a six-pack, weed, a pocketful of pharmaceuticals,
      two gringas from San Diego. Instead of the sun, it was the moon.
Another log thrown on the bonfire of my senses. Howler monkeys
      serenading. Stars crackling in all directions: nature's chandelier.
I wanted something authentic, something I could feel in my bones.
Now, on top of the same pyramid, in a Mayan city, swallowed
      down the jungle's green throat a thousand years ago,
I stare out at a giant Ceiba. Its top branches covered
      in a fur-like substance, erupting out like spider arms,
      so it looks as if a tarantula has mated with the tree.
I'm searching for a metaphor to connect the old and new me.
My wife of two weeks and I walk the Tikal forest, clear pearls of sweat
      jewelling our foreheads.
A throng of monkeys frenzying between limbs barely resembles
      me and my teenage friends on a street corner drinking binge.
The freshly shed skin of a mud-colored snake one-quarter reminds me
      of the life I wriggled out of.
An ocelot nimble on a branch, like how my id purred—ah,
      none of these metaphors are working.
Then I see a tree, a strangler fig, Ficus aurea, prince of the dark forest,
      literally enveloping another, coiling the length of its trunk,
      its roots shooting up and down, choking the life out.

Legacy is a piece of toilet paper hanging out of your pants at a family reunion

You wake and find yellow traffic signs
with silhouettes of your face
plastered around the neighborhood.

The night before is scattered at your feet
like the shattered side window of a dump truck.

The mind is a carpet, and memories
are all the crap you can't scrub up,
like those nights as a kid with your mom,
watching home movies of your Irish ancestors
wash up on Ellis Island in their speedboats.

On the outside of a milk carton
is the name and face of your inner child.
On the inside of the carton is printed
the child's whereabouts.

Yes, you were born the black sheep of the family.
Yes, your parents shaved off your wool coat
to pay for your brother's piano lessons.

Yes, reality is a bemusement park
you're not allowed to leave, so spin
cotton candy from the strands
of your dead grandmother's hair,

and smile when you look at the sky—
someone really is laughing up there.

The High Heat

Hovering over a plate of spumoni in the kitchen,
I grip the handle of my spoon. A hundred miles away,
in public housing for seniors, my mother sets,
twirls into her windup, cocks her arm back
and unleashes a wad of bills, that she can't pay,
from a Home Shopping Network binge,
miraculously amassed without a credit card.
The pitch zooms up and in. The whiskers
quiver on my chin. *I told you no more
curve balls, mom.* I kick my spikes into the wood floor.
But I'm a curve ball pitcher, she says, adjusting her cap.

Kicking the Lust Bucket

Rising in a café
in Pittsburgh,
I feel a man's eyes
press into my chest
as I slide an arm
into my overcoat.
I do not recoil
from his wounded gaze,
like when I was twelve
hustling home,
wet-haired,
from swim practice,
men perched on corners
in tight pants, eyes
rolling around
in their heads,
like the steel balls
on roulette wheels.
Cars prowling
in engorged circles,
thorned eyes peering
through smeared windshields
at my porcelain cheeks.
I do not recoil
from the hunger
in the man's eyes,
the look that is ¾ pain
and ¼ desire, like his foot

is clamped in a steel trap,
and his eyes are begging
for release. I do not judge
the man his hunger,
but I do not lean
into it either, do not
sprinkle a thimble
of kerosene into his broiled
heat just to watch
his face flame up
and flicker. I remember
an old landlord in California,
planting jonquils
in the common soil
between our doors,
his sinewy, shirtless
chest, tattoos roving
across his skin glisten,
how I tilted a hip,
conjured a blush,
wondered if my lip
taunt made the broken
glass in his loin
reassemble
into a bottle
I might feign
to sip from. I button
my coat. I can't

help this man. Even
if I bent over
and wrapped
my hands around
his swollen purple
foot and released it
from that shark-jaw
tension, it wouldn't
help. Lust is a bucket
that never stays filled.
A drop always spills,
and all the bucket feels
is the absence of that drop,
radiating outward
like the phantom throb
of a permanently
popping capillary.

Youngest Brother Turning Forty

I want to say something insightful, like *you're halfway there
on life's circular journey*, but life is more like a Jackson Pollock:

little bits of experience randomly splattered
over the canvas of your senses. I want to say something clever,

like *if feelings were permanent, tears would stain our clothing like blood*,
but the fact is feelings seep inward, into the fabric of our spleens.

I want to say something wise, like *never submit your first emotional draft
for publication*, but the fact is both of our mouths spring open

and shut impulsively, like mouse traps built into our faces.
I want a sentence firm enough to pat myself on the back,

like *despite it all I've been a good brother*, but the fact is
we were never each other's favorites, and the ledger

of aggressions can not be wiped clean. I'll always be the one
who sold you pot when you were twelve, at double the price,

the one who crowned you with a bowl of cereal. I want to say
something useful, like *the trick is seeing the world through stained-glass pupils*,

but some nights the mirror looks as dark as the bags under mom's eyes
each morning at the breakfast table, as if all the pills

she'd been popping had clumped into a hand in her brain,
and the hand was applying makeup from within.

Fifty-Fifty Ball

Yesterday, I was cruising along, behind the wheel,
listening to that song "Age of Consent" by New Order,
and I swear—twenty-five years of my life just up and flew
out the window, like a hot dog wrapper. Whole chunks of me
are breaking off. The referee blows the halftime whistle.
Coach yells, *locker room*, so I take off my shin guards,
go in, but there's no one there, just me
and all these empty lockers filled with the bones of kids
I went to grade school with. Coach yells, *back on the field.*
Suck it up. Be a man, but I just feel like wearing lipstick
and writing the words *god's slut* on my forehead. Why
is life this itchy pair of socks I yearn to remove each night,
so I can run around naked in someone else's skin?

Half-breed

Throw a Frisbee and all day
I'll bark after it, paws churning
up dirt, lungs pumping, tail
swagging, as I loft and glide
and snatch the plastic disc
of approval, but I will not
lie at your feet, even when petted,
even when you work your fingers
through my freshly groomed fur.
Look deeper, and you'll find
evidence of my mangy roots.
Look between my teeth and see
slithers of skin from the hand
that fed me. Half purebred,
half bitch. How they tied me
out in the rain all night,
sculpting a howl, dodging
apples hurled from cars.

Cleaves

The phrase *memory bank* is false—you can't slip a plastic card
into the side of your head and make a withdrawal.

There's no cashier, but maybe there's a vault behind your irises,
with a green lock, and a brass door leading to a warehouse,

with aisles filled with boxes, arranged by year. Some boxes
contain dioramas of rooms you woke up in, blow-up dolls

of girls you almost kissed, like Aegean-eyed Maya, a series
of bummed cigarettes, then back to her place for tea,

a light green bra on the pillow. See how slippery
her skin still is? Why didn't you walk through the door

she carved in the air and handed you the key to?
Why didn't you chomp the peach she dipped in chamomile

and brushed across your teeth? One day, it'll be just you,
strapped to a helium balloon, floating through the darkness,

halfway to Jupiter, clutching memories to your ribcage,
as if the details of your shed life could shield you

from the stars glittering like the tips of frozen cigarettes
in the firing squad's lips, as if recollecting the name

of that prune-faced third-grade teacher,
who never liked you, could somehow ward off

the cold-skinned beast, with numerals for eyes,
ripping childhood drawings off the walls of your mind.

**poem beginning with a line from Bob Dylan's
"Subterranean Homesick Blues"**
for Gary Close

Ah get born, keep warm,
short pants, romance, learn to dance
circles around the jackals
in their polyester grievances,
hawking fool's neon,
like fake watches strapped
inside a huckster's overcoat.
Hop, on the boxcar, baby,
we're hitting the ri-zoad,
like a bottle of Martian whisky.
Last week a cop held a radar gun
to my cranium, said my thoughts
were going ninety-four miles an hour
over the speed limit. Lately
I've been seeing men with shovels
lurking behind trees, smoking cigarillos
waiting to seal me in a maple envelope
and mail me to the mud.
The giant clock on the moon
says I have seven thousand
and four days to live. Last week
I watched the shovel men slide
a kid I grew up with, now forty-five,
into the ground, then start piling dirt
when the last taillight of his loved ones
flickered away. Gary, you fro-headed,
no-dancing, spiral-tossing white boy,

with a Phillies flag in your casket.
You full-moon-of-teeth smiling,
leader-of-our-stoop-hanging
22nd and Lombard crew,
with your cutoff mesh T-shirts
and ready-for-take-off tube socks
and *three Mississippis* in a parking lot.
You malt-liquor swilling, 8-ball sinking,
drum-stick breaking, Taney-hating,
laying all still in your silk box
in the cancerous skin that betrayed you,
the word *daddy* on a banner. At the gravesite,
your wife and daughters cried like birds
guarding the entrance of the underworld,
and your soul was little chunks of bread
being pried from their mouths
as the shovel men dropped you
down the chute to Hades. Keep warm
down there, skip the romance.
If you get reborn, this time
learn to dance.

Mapache

Two-lane country road, sixty-five
miles an hour, moonlight
sprinkling ivory petals on asphalt.
A raccoon bolts from a hedge.
Slam the brakes. Screech. Whap.
Plastic bumper of my hybrid cracked.

In a dream, when an enemy appears,
they say it's a dark version of your self,
a chance for your two halves to meet.
Who did that raccoon represent?
What rogue part of my psyche?

The raccoon emerges. I accelerate.
Die you filthy bastard, you dirty letch,
with those creepy porno eyeballs
and black circles, like you've been playing
bull's-eyes with body parts all night.

That raccoon charged out of my id,
and now it's costing me five hundred
smackers, I think, hanging up
with the insurance.

Mom, Dad, whoever's up in those clouds,
why do I need this id? Why didn't it fall off
at forty, like the booster of a rocket ship?

I run my finger through the skull dent
in the fender. Dense underfur provides insulation
from the frosty eyeball of public opinion.

Mapache, I feel you prowling the night.
lumbering onto my trash can, up on hind legs,
staring into the matrimony window,
your sprung rudder pulsing in your hand,
five times more sensitive than lips.

Middle Age

After an hour on the phone with creditors,
your testosterone feels like watered-down lemonade.

You couldn't impregnate an awkward pause. Remember
the old days, when your wife was belly swollen,

and you strutted Brooklyn streets with an internal boner
twanging against your spleen, imagined being a crop duster

filled with semen and pollinating all the women
passing in springtime dungarees. Now you clean

greasy spots of masculinity off the tiles, and mop
on your knees like Cinderella, with saggy boobs

and a T-shirt that says *used to be one of the fellas.* Now
the bathroom feels just way too biological.

Even in your man cave, you're civilized: to-do lists
spray-painted on the ceiling. A latex doll

wobbles towards you, holding a strap-on
and a palm full of Rogaine.

undocumented joyrider in the land of the flesh

I'm running up a hillside that's covered in crabgrass,
burrowing under bushes, that undulate like a pair of hips,
as god's spotlight lashes down, so I cover my limbs
with sulfur and paprika, to blend in with the dirt. I'm illegal here,
in the land of pleasure, and I know it. Hiding from god,
like he's *la migre*, is no way to spend a Saturday. If he catches
whiff of me, I'll be deported from this privileged land of touch.

Excuse me, senor fuckface,
sorry to interrupt your poem,
but you just can't grab any subject
and turn it into a metaphor
to describe your spiritual pain.
I don't care if your wife
and daughter are Hispanic.
The border isn't some jump rope
for you to play hopscotch with.
It's not a tightrope strung between
flagpoles that people walk
barefooted and blindfolded
over safety nets of broken glass.

I'm ready for you, Lord. It's me, Senor Fuckface. Tie me down
with your jump rope and drag broken glass over my metaphors,
till the little demon inside me, tight-roping between my earlobes,
takes off his safety net blindfold and shows his true face.

Reckoning

Where are you right now, emotionally?
I'm back in the fourth grade,
telling the teacher *bathroom.*

I'm in the stall, on the toilet,
my pants still zipped,
wondering if my absence

has become visible.
Minutes crawl by like a tick
up the school nurse's thigh.

There's a world out there:
a teacher with a black book,
bullied siblings, a glum wife.

And where are you?
I'm here—carving
a space out of emptiness,

a closet out of thin air.
Do you believe in god?
I believe I'm being punished

by something external
for wrongs I've committed,
and my punishment includes:

leaning down to pick up
a quarter and banging my skull
on a door handle; a hundred-

and-three degree fever,
like a long, thin stop sign
shooting up the thermometer's spine;

this coughing so hard,
like receiving an unlicensed
chiropractic adjustment

from within, but I'm thankful
for each fist of salt
scrubbed into my wounds.

I don't want to get away with it
anymore. Getting away with it
is the worst punishment of all.

Yard Work

Sixty degrees and sunny, mid-March,
an ambivalent wind coaxing raked leaves
loose from flowerbeds. I'm at the overgrown hedge,
gripping a limb cutter. Snow-weighted branches
curve down into a dull, monochromatic rainbow.
I'm hacking the branches down to the stem
so the bush can live, so its leaves can flourish
and protect us from the eyes of neighbors.
I stretch up and slash a defiant bough,
wrapped in the arms of the wisteria, coiled
around a drainpipe, and think of me and my first
girlfriend: two malnourished, rootless things
clinging to one another and calling it love.
I wince and hack deeper into the bramble.
A pile of severed branches waist-high. Thorns
tug at my sleeves. The truest version
of love I ever saw was a pair of palm trees,
twenty feet apart, tall and dignified
in the desert sky, their leaves brushing
when wind conspired towards them,
their roots touching like toes underground.

Chapel of Inadvertent Joy

One minute you're hissing at your wife about something trivial,
the next you're stomping derelict train tracks, when it emerges,

its spires shooting up between your ribs,
your gaze swivels skyward and catches a clutch of birds,

glittering over a smokestack, sparkling back and forth in the sky,
in various formations, like a math equation being worked out

in the mind of a genius. Always pull the car over when you spot
a teen punk rock show at dusk in a public park. Always drink

a glimpse of a white horse in a sunlit pasture at the end of summer.
Always laugh when the garden hose slips out of your hand

and sprays you in the face. When they said *smell the roses*,
they didn't tell you that every day the rose changes,

that first you must identify the rose. Today you're in a field
by the Hudson. Ribbons of nectar spool from a folk singer's lips,

your wife and daughter lollygag in the grass. Sunlight
drizzles through tree leaves, an organic stained-glass window.

Feel the convergence of all your stray voltage. Don't pull out
of that feeling. Let the father standing next to you

see your eyes well up, the inverse of how the neighbors
sometimes hear you yelling *fuck*. It's true—you don't deserve this,

but it's yours anyway: the gold-tipped spurs of this moment,
a red bird flinging praise through the sky.

Acknowledgments

Thanks to the editors of the following publications, where earlier versions of the following poems first appeared:

"Track of Now," "*Mapache*," "Hello," "Fifty-Fifty Ball," and "A Brief History of Immortality" appeared in *American Poetry Review*; "Elliot Spitzer in Grad School," "The High Heat," and "Legacy is a piece of toilet paper hanging out of your pants at a family reunion" appeared in *A Poetry Congeries, Connotations Press: An Online Artifact*; "Keeper of the Light," "The Cuckold Explores the Subjunctive," and "Satan Exulting Over Eve" appeared in *B O D Y*; "Holiday Weekend," "from *The Cuckold's Survival Manual*," and "Lust in Translation" appeared in *Columbia Poetry Review*; "Happy Marriage" and "Attention, Please" appeared in *Crab Orchard Review*; "Queen of the Shortcuts" appeared in *Field*; "Return to *El Perdido Mundo*" appeared in *Gulf Coast*; "The Barbecued Man" and "A Brief History of the Future" appeared in the *Nashville Review*; "undocumented joyrider in the land of the flesh" and "The Cuckold and the Penal System" appeared in *No Comment*; "Chapel of Inadvertent Joy," "I Am Not an Idiot," "Half-Breed," and "The Cuckold in Autumn" appeared in *The Operating System*; "The Cuckold Sees the Bigger Picture," "Life as a Donkey," "Interview with a Cuckold," and "Middle Age" appeared in *Pear Noir*; "Conditionals," "Pity Party," and "Reflections of a Cuckold and Other Blasphemies" appeared in *Ping Pong*; "The Birds and the Bees" and "Beware of the Dark Sedan" appeared in *Ploughshares*; "The Furies" appeared in *Sixteen*; "The Grudge," "poem beginning with a line from Bob Dylan's 'Subterranean Homesick Blues,'" "Kicking the Lust

Bucket," and "A Brief History of Neon" appeared in *Sonora Review*; "Reckoning" and *"Cleaves"* appeared in *Southern California Review*; "Keeper of the Light," "Youngest Brother Turning Forty," and "A Brief History of Eyebrows" appeared in *S T I L L: Magazin fur junge Literatur & Fotografe*; "The Cougar Tree," "Pick-up Lines of the Marquis de Sade," and "The Cuckold Contemplates the Malibu Fires" appeared in *Stone Cutter*; "Little Soldier of Love" and "Yard Work" appeared in the *Sugarhouse Review*.

"The Grudge" was reprinted in *Best American Poetry 2010*, edited by Amy Gerstler.

"Conditionals" and "Queen of the Shortcuts" were reprinted in *Der Greif* (Germany), December 2011, edited by Lydia Daher.

"poem beginning with a line from Bob Dylan's 'Subterranean Homesick Blues'" grew out of a poetic challenge devised by Roddy Lumsden. Various poets were randomly given lines from "Subterranean Homesick Blues" to be used as an opening.

"Satan Exulting Over Eve" is based on William Blake's drawing of the same name. The poem was presented at the Getty Museum of Art in Los Angeles in September 2011, in conjunction with the Dark Blushing exhibit, curated by Mindy Netifee and Amber Tamblyn.

Thank you to Amy Gerstler and Kendra DeColo for reading earlier drafts of this book and providing valuable feedback.

Thank you to Drew O'Leary and David Morrison for your decades of friendship and support. May your spirits be free of the burdens of this world.